Parenting Matters:

Raising Successful Kids

Parenting Matters:

Raising Successful Kids

Margaret Roane

Copyright © 2012 by Margaret Roane.

To Ruth and Melford Walker and Norman and Lillye Roane, and all of the other "old school" parents whose methods my husband and I did our best to emulate, and to whom we owe an eternal debt of gratitude for shaping us into the people we are today.

To George, Randy and Joseph, the joys of our lives. Thanks for all the wonderful experiences and memories we share. We love you!

And to our Heavenly Father, who has given us the grace to walk out our parenting journey. There are just no words to express our appreciation!

Contents

Introduction	9
Essential Parenting Guidelines	13
Infancy	23
Toddlerhood	31
Preschoolers	39
Elementary School Age	45
Tweens (Middle School)	59
Teens (High School)	73
College and Beyond	85
Parenting in a Nutshell	91
Frequently Asked Questions	95
Topical Index	99

Introduction

Welcome to the most important, most challenging job you'll ever have – raising your child! Sometimes new parents are overwhelmed with the enormity and complexity of the task ahead; children don't come with instruction manuals! This book can be your road map into the exciting journey that awaits.

I'd like to start by saying that there are many ways to successfully raise children – my purpose and goal is simply to share what has worked for my husband and me. Let me also be the first to admit that we were not perfect parents; as all parents do, we made our share of mistakes along the way. Nor did we raise perfect children – they are human, too. My hope is that something said in this book will help parents make the best choices they can while performing an underrated but pivotal role in our society and our world. Very often, parents receive little to no public recognition for

Introduction

their efforts and sacrifices; don't let the lack of appreciation by the outside world deter you! In my job as a school counselor, I have the opportunity to complement dedicated parents, and I love to do so! Raising successful, well-adjusted children is not easy, but it is a very worthwhile goal, and it can be done if parenting your children is one of your top priorities in time and effort.

My husband and I both have worked in education for many years. We have seen wonderful young people whose parents made great choices, and we have seen the wasted potential of children whose parents made less desirable choices. As a school counselor, I have seen that many of the problems parents face at the high school level can be attributed to a lack of proper discipline and structure during the child's formative years. My fondest hope is that future parents will find inspiration in these pages to make those tough choices to help their children be the best they can be and achieve their life dreams.

In this book we will explore the concept of raising a *functional, independent, contributing adult.* Most parents want their

Introduction

children to grow up with the ability to *function* in our world, which will require a myriad of skills not present at birth, such as walking, talking, toileting control, reading, writing, mathematical and organizational skills, and getting along with others, to name a few! Parents also want their children to make a *contribution* to the world as adults, usually through their careers. And even the most loving parents look forward to the day their children become self-supporting and *independent*, moving out of the family home into a place of their own. This book will guide parents through the process of developing the skills necessary to follow this progression.

Finally, remember that prayer is an essential component in your journey; pray often for your children, their future, and their choices, and for your own wisdom, patience, and unconditional parental love. If you haven't been a believer in the power of prayer, this difficult journey will help you get there!

Parenting Matters: Raising Successful Kids

Chapter One: Essential Parenting Guidelines

It seems like yesterday when my now-grown sons were infants, toddlers, preschoolers, school agers, tweens, and teens. I blinked, it seems, and they became wonderful grown men. Although my journey in retrospect seems much too short, I treasure many memories of their childhood days. My goal is to share with today's parents some of the lessons gained in thirty-plus years of parenting. Let's begin with some basic principles:

Lesson I: Child-rearing is a long-term project.

"Train up a child in the way he should go: and when he is old, he will not depart from it" (Proverbs 22:6).

Parenting Matters: Raising Successful Kids

Although it is hard to believe, your curly-haired, bright-eyed child will also be a teenager and then an adult very quickly. Always weigh the long-term effects of your parenting decisions, keeping in mind the ultimate goal of raising a *functional, independent, contributing adult.* Children will not be children forever; while it may be tempting to let them do whatever they choose, have whatever they want, and behave however they wish, such parenting choices will result in long-term regrets. It is our job as parents to teach our children how to live in our society. Some parents mistakenly attempt to keep 'Junior' happy 24 hours a day by letting him do as he chooses, even if it is a poor choice, such as eating candy for breakfast or throwing his food on the floor. Don't trade temporary happiness for long-term gain!

Like any long-term project, parenting will require a considerable amount of your time, resources, and energy. Remember, love is spelled T-I-M-E. No amount of money will eventually substitute for giving your child your time and attention. The transition from being a couple to being parents is most dramatically felt in the demands on your time. Your "me" time and your couple time will shrink considerably when your child is born, and will not return to pre-baby levels until your child is grown and gone (at least off to college!). What's best for your child will often require a sacrifice from the parents especially in terms of money and time. Make your mind up now to put in the time necessary for this long-term project; it will be the best investment you will ever make.

<u>Lesson II</u>: Establish your authority while your child is young.

"Children, obey your parents in the Lord: for this is right" (Ephesians 6:1).

As a parent, it is essential to establish parental authority, assert it whenever necessary, and reassert it when the inevitable challenges come. Those who ignore this basic truth will live to regret it when the tumultuous teenage years arrive! Respect for authority – parental authority, school authority, and the rule of law in society – is easiest to teach when children are young; it is extremely difficult to "crack down on" a teenager who has become accustomed to ignoring your authority. Using the rewards and consequences of your choice, you must train your child to do what you say! I remember when my youngest son was about a year old, the age when children are not talking much but understand you perfectly well. My husband was in the family room watching him, and my son decided to leave the room. My husband told him to stay in the room, and my son put one foot across the threshold and looked back at my husband to see if he really meant what he said. My husband, a firm believer in parental discipline, rose to the challenge, as further discussed in Lesson IV.

Your child will not understand or agree with many of your rules and decisions, and he/she will need to learn to comply with your decisions regardless of their opinions. Please note that this training begins even before your child can talk. In addition to making your home life more harmonious, discipline and respect for authority are basic requirements for functioning in a civilized society. Our correctional facilities are filled with people who choose to disregard authority; don't let your child be numbered among them. Respect for authority is a lesson best learned early from one's parents in the home.

Lesson III: Happiness is a well-behaved child.

"Even a child is known by his doings, whether his work be pure, and whether it be right" (Proverbs 20:11).

Many parents mistakenly believe that their job is to ensure that their child is happy every moment of every day. Not so! If you are teaching your child correct behavior and establishing discipline and authority in his/her life, there will certainly be times when he/she is unhappy with your choices and the consequences you prescribe. Stand firm - you are on the right track! While every parent should take steps to provide things for and do things with his/her child to make them happy, this does not mean that your child should exist only in a constant state of happiness. Just hearing the word "No" will make some children unhappy ☺. Some parents fear that they will lose their child's love if they make the child unhappy by saying "No" or by punishing the child for misbehavior. In large measure, this is an unfounded fear; as they grow older, children sense that permissive parents really don't care enough about their children to set and enforce limits and boundaries.

In the long run, children are very forgiving, and they will appreciate your efforts on their behalf. One evening I was working with my youngest son on his math homework, and I was giving him a hard time because he had not put forth a good effort. A friend of my middle son heard me fussing, and I was embarrassed until she said, "I wish someone had worked with me like that when I was younger." Temporary unhappiness, like the discomfort we may feel during a tough workout, is fine if we as parents are working towards a greater good.

Remember that your goal is to raise a *functional, independent, contributing adult*. There will be times when you must choose between what your child wants to do and what is best for him/her – make the right choice! Being a good parent is hard work; even if your child says "I hate you" and holds a momentary grudge when you stand your ground, it is far better to raise a well-behaved child that is mad with you than to raise a hooligan who is crazy about you!

Lesson IV: Discipline is not the enemy of enthusiasm.

"Foolishness is bound in the heart of a child; but the rod of correction shall drive it far from him" (Proverbs 22:15).

At the risk of upsetting many as we begin our journey, I will mention that I believe in spanking children. My husband and I found that a few swats to the bottom, taps on the legs, or a pinch helped our kids understand that certain actions would not be tolerated. I understand that many parents today are hesitant to physically discipline their children, but based on my experience and observations, "time outs" and other such methods do not seem to be nearly as effective. Spanking is most useful with younger children, and is needed less and less as children get older; indeed, once your children know that you will spank them, just the threat of spanking will often be sufficient to discourage their undesirable behaviors. This concept is known in parenting circles as "the look". Parents would witness that our kids would stop misbehaving when we made eye contact with them in public settings, and they would ask my husband and me how to achieve "the look"; we informed them that "the look" was preceded by "the spanking"! As children get older and have more privileges, especially for tweens and teens, there are a wide variety of effective consequences for parents to use to shape their children's behavior, such as grounding them, taking their cell phones (if you decide to get them one), and taking the car keys!

Some parents, hesitant to discipline their children, try to use encouragement, praise, and redirection exclusively to direct their child's behavior. Encouragement and praise are certainly essential for parents to give to their children, as long as the praise is deserved and sincere; redirection is very useful as well, especially for younger children. Be warned, however, that these techniques are no substitute for discipline, especially when your child directly and blatantly disobeys your instructions. Real parental love requires that both discipline and encouragement be given to the child as needed.

Essential Parenting Guidelines

Whatever method of discipline you choose, it is important to be consistent and persistent. It is also important to follow through on promised punishments; this is easier when parents assign realistic consequences to begin with, as opposed to those chosen in the heat of anger, such as, "You can't go outside any more this summer!" If you don't follow through on promised consequences, you quickly lose credibility with your children. The goal of your discipline is to teach your children to control their behavior; this discipline is the root of the self-control they will need to have to be successful in whatever endeavors they pursue in their adult lives.

Now, let's examine how these guiding principles can be applied to each stage of development. Whether you are an expectant parent or well on your journey through parenthood, there's something here for you. Read on, and I wish you the very best as you do your most important job of all – raise your child.

Chapter Two: Infancy

Baby's First Days

The first task for new parents is to attend to their infant's basic needs. Feed the baby when he is hungry, change her when she is wet, and comfort him when he cries. It is positive for babies to receive prompt care. And feel free to hold your child – she needs your loving touch! But have the baby sleep in his own bed, not yours; this is a safety issue so that you don't smother the baby, and it is the beginning of the *independence* that is our long-term goal for the child. Some parents say they just fall asleep unintentionally with the baby in the parent's bed; try putting a rocking chair in the nursery and feed the baby there. It is preferable for baby to sleep in her own room; the parents will actually be able to rest, instead of wakening with the baby's every wiggle or sigh.

Then, here is the magic step: do not hold the child until he falls asleep; lay her down at night or at naptime and let him put himself to sleep. Again, we are moving the child towards *independence* even at this early stage! Lay the child down, give her a pat, tell her goodnight, and leave the room. If he cries when you leave, wait a few minutes, return to the room, pat and soothe him without picking him up, and leave again. Repeat as necessary until the baby falls asleep. Eventually the baby will put herself to sleep without a fuss. Amazing, right? Parents who only put children down once they are asleep live to regret it, and have to perform this process with more difficulty when the child is older.

Whether you breast or bottle feed your child, you may want to consider giving the 2 am feeding using a bottle (of breast milk or formula, your choice), so that both parents can share the late night feeding. That way Mom can get a little sleep and Dad has an opportunity to bond with the baby, especially important if the baby is breast-fed. Also, whenever parents choose to wean the baby from breastfeeding, the baby is already accustomed to taking the bottle and weaning is easier. Many doctors recommend that babies drink milk from a cup when they are a year old; certainly by a year old, if not much sooner, the baby should be sleeping through the night without feedings (and we should note that two year olds do *not* need a 2 am feeding – they should be eating enough solid food at dinner to sleep through the night!). Another tip for the nighttime feedings is to keep them brief, with dim lighting; encourage interaction and play during the daytime feedings with bright lighting, so that the little one will get the idea that night is for sleeping and day is for play!

Dad's Involvement

Please note that Dad will have his own method of feeding, changing diapers, bathing, carrying, and playing with the baby. Mom, please don't interfere! It's perfectly fine for Dad to interact with the baby in his own way. Fathers and mothers often differ in their approach to parenting; usually, neither parent is right all the time, and a compromise or blending of styles provides the balance of nurturing and challenge that is often the best result for the child. For example, I loved picking my children up and carrying them around because they wanted to be held and I wanted to hold them; however, my husband encouraged them to walk more once they were able to do so, building strength and endurance as well as *independence*.

Parenting Matters: Raising Successful Kids

This may not be conclusive proof that he was right, but all three boys were standout track and field athletes in high school, so I guess it didn't hurt them either!

As baby begins to sleep all night, a pattern of naptimes, playtimes, and bedtime will emerge. The structure provided through a regular routine makes life easier for both parents and children. My favorite time of the day was the bedtime routine of bathtime (with me singing songs from my childhood), a bedtime story or two, goodnight prayers, and sweet dreams. Routines will ease your child into bedtime without a fuss, and create precious memories for both of you.

Independent Play

The next challenge as the baby gets older is independent play. Especially by the time the baby sits up on its own, have it play in a playpen or on a blanket independently with soft toys while the parent attends to chores. This allows the child to learn to entertain itself, another step toward *independence*. A playpen or pack-and-

Infancy

play ensures the child's safety during independent play time as the child begins to crawl, and the child can improve motor skills by pulling up and walking around the edges. Not to mention, this gives busy parents a much-needed breather in the day to relax or do chores while the child is awake. I have heard parents say, "My child won't stay in the playpen without crying." My husband says, "Did the child make a rope ladder out of his blanket and climb out?" ☺ The baby may cry at first when left to its own devices. Just as when she learned to fall asleep independently, follow the same rules; let her cry for a few moments, comfort her without picking her up, withdraw, and repeat.

You may say, "Wait a minute! First you said to comfort the baby when he cries, and now you say to let him cry sometimes – I'm confused!" As a new parent, you will quickly learn to distinguish cries of genuine need (e.g. hunger or pain) from more manipulative crying (e.g. I don't want to go to sleep now, I don't want to entertain myself, I want every toy I see in the store, I want that knife you won't let me play with, etc., - a list that will grow longer until the baby is older and talks fluently). The key is to respond to genuine needs and not to let the baby or toddler control you by crying. Babies and toddlers are quite smart, and although they can't talk yet, they are adept at getting what they want by crying. Be warned and remember to establish your authority. You determine where the baby sleeps, when bedtime is, and other parental choices – do not hand over your authority to the child, because you are going to need it in this parenting journey!

Also note that some parents resist independence in their children; perhaps because of deep-seated needs of their own, they want the baby to bond only with them, to cry whenever they put him down, to sleep with them, and to breastfeed much longer than is recommended. Please consider what is best for the child as you raise him/her, not just what is pleasurable or gratifying for the parent. Remember our goal – a *functional, independent, contributing adult*. Letting go and moving to the next phase can be difficult for the parents, but the long-term rewards are worth the struggle.

The idea of *independence* when talking about an infant may seem a little strange to some. Remember that we are on a journey,

Infancy

and that your baby will not be a baby for very long. An independent baby sleeps in his own bed and in his own room, can put himself to sleep, and can entertain himself at play. An independent toddler will walk on her own and learn to use the potty, while an independent preschooler can dress herself and brush her own teeth. Before you know it, you will have an independent college student that can manage his own money, keep up with his assignments, projects, and deadlines, do his own laundry and keep his dorm room (relatively) neat and clean. But independence, like the other qualities we are developing, does not just happen on its own; we are taking baby steps all along our journey.

Chapter Three: Toddlerhood

When raising toddlers, it is important to remember that they understand what you say long before they are actually able to speak at all, not to mention before they speak in sentences or complete thoughts. And as they start to walk and run, it is imperative that they learn to obey your voice (e.g. "Don't run into the street!"). If they don't follow your directions, punishment should ensue; repeat until they stop when told to do so. I am aware that this may seem harsh, but the child's safety and its very life may be at stake. In addition, remember that you are continuing to establish your parental authority in the home, and that you will periodically have to reestablish that authority as your child moves through its stages of development.

Another area of concern at this stage is discouraging bad habits your toddler develops. These can range from pinching, biting, and hitting to throwing his/her food at dinnertime. Consistent reprimands or punishments will reduce the duration of these behaviors. When one of my sons was small, he adopted the habit of pinching people. He pinched both of his grandmothers; one of them spanked his hand, and the other laughed and thought it was cute. You can imagine which grandmother continued to receive pinches!

Temper Tantrums

Before you know it, the "terrible two's" will be upon you. How will you handle them? It is up to you to help your child continue to move forward in her development. The hallmark of the terrible two's is the famed temper tantrum, where the child falls to the floor, crying because he/she did not get his/her way. Parents vary on how they handle this; my husband punished the behavior, and I ignored it by leaving the scene of the tantrum. Both methods can be successful – the important thing is not to give in to the tantrum and let the child have or do what she wants. Caving in to the tantrum only reinforces the behavior; if the child is successful using the tantrum, why would he change behaviors? Teach your child how to properly ask for what she wants, and be aware that she still will not like hearing "No" for an answer. In such situations,

Toddlerhood

redirection is a wonderful thing! Refocus the child on something else entirely, and further crying and angst can often be averted. Another trick of the trade with toddlers (and with older kids too) is to give them a choice between two appropriate options; sometimes just having a choice can be very satisfying to the child.

There are two schools of thought on whether all fragile items should be removed from your home because you have small children. Some folks feel it is best to remove the items and avoid any controversy over what the child can touch; others feel it is reasonable to teach the child not to bother certain items. We had the best success with moving dangerous or breakable items out of the child's reach where possible (e.g. scissors, glass items, medicines, etc.), and teaching the child not to bother items that could not reasonably be moved (e.g. stereo equipment, televisions, etc.). I have a statuette on an end table in my den, and my little grandson knows it is mine and to leave it alone. His dad picked up the statuette and my grandson said, "Daddy, don't play with that – that's Grandma's!" You will be amazed at what you can accomplish with loving correction and redirection.

Parenting Matters: Raising Successful Kids

Toddler Do's

Here are some "do's" for you and your toddler:

- Do read to your toddler every day to foster language development.

- Do talk in complete sentences, no "baby talk", for the same reason.

- Do take your child on interesting, fun, and educational outings to expose him/her to the wide, wide world.

- Do offer healthy meals and snacks, realizing that their appetites will vary.

- Do limit snacks just before mealtimes – children have small stomachs!

- Do participate in physical activities with your child – walks, the playground, catch – to encourage motor skill development and foster an active lifestyle.

- Do minimize stroller usage for a toddler that walks well for the same reason, and to encourage *independence*.

- Do carry toys, books, and snacks when you are out with your toddler, especially when waiting is involved. A toddler cannot sit quietly doing nothing and wait patiently like an adult can. Be sure you have a survival kit of amusements and goodies with you, especially when travelling. You don't want to have a bored, hungry, crying child on a long airplane flight – your fellow airline passengers will thank you!!

- Do continue to provide routine and structure for your toddler; regular naptimes, bedtimes, and mealtimes provide a sense of security and make for a more manageable child. There's nothing like hearing a crying child in the store whose naptime or bedtime has been ignored! Plan your schedule around your child's naptime and bedtime, and everyone's days will be better.

- Do begin the process of teaching your child to dress himself/herself. He/she will surprise you with how quickly they learn this skill if you patiently, consistently work on it each day and night. Allow extra time in the mornings for this process! The same goes for your child brushing his/her teeth both morning and night – it's time to start those good hygiene habits.

- Do encourage your child to feed himself, even if the process is a little messy at first – again we are working towards *independence.*
- Do get yourself ready in the mornings before your child arises; this one tip will really smooth out the morning rush!

Potty Training

Potty training is another milestone in this stage of development; it is also a big step toward becoming a *functional, independent, contributing adult.* Recommendations vary on when to begin, but we used the second birthday as a starting point. One child we knew would go get a clean diaper when she was wet – that's a child that's ready to start potty training! ☺ Little boys often like to "make bubbles" in the toilet, and can be sent to the toilet with an older sibling so they get the general idea of what is expected.

Ready to get started? Buy your child some "big boy/girl" underwear with his favorite characters on them, and start using them during daytime hours. Have your child use the potty as soon as she gets up in the morning and after naptime, after each meal, and before naptime and bedtime. Remember that this is a process and there will be accidents. Don't fuss or berate your child when they happen; simply wash him/her off and change to clean clothing. Praise and encourage your child when he successfully uses the potty. Control of bowel movements normally precedes control of urination, and daytime control precedes nighttime control. Continue at first to use diapers or pull-ups at night, when traveling, and for public occasions (e.g. church, parties, etc.). When your child wakes up consistently with dry diapers, go for nighttime control as well. Your patience and consistency will be rewarded, and your child will be potty trained before you know it. Congratulations!

This is also the time many children visit the doctor and dentist for the first time. It is important for parents to model confidence and calm for these events instead of fear. The same is true for occasions when children fall down or otherwise injure themselves; when you as the parent remain calm, your child will also do so.

Parenting Matters: Raising Successful Kids

Chapter Four: Preschoolers

During the preschool years, the parenting focus shifts to more academic pursuits. Since your child was a toddler or younger, you have been reading to your child; continue to do so on a daily basis. The names of facial features, major body parts, and everyday objects should also be part of your child's vocabulary, along with colors, numbers, shapes, days of the week, months of the year, animals, plants, and any other interesting items your child likes; one of our favorite books for this purpose was, "The Biggest Word Book Ever". Use every opportunity you can as a teachable moment to name new objects and activities; walks in the neighborhood and trips to the mall can be great teaching times for parents. Flash cards or computer games that teach letters and sounds are also very useful for preschoolers. We purchased workbooks and other materials to work with our children before they began formal schooling; also, consider enrolling your child in preschool and head start programs to improve your child's kindergarten readiness.

Parenting Matters: Raising Successful Kids

Why?

This is also the time, more than any other, when you will be asked, "Why?" It can be annoying to hear this question so much, but remember to patiently explain "why" as often as possible when your child asks. He or she is anxious to learn and reason, and this is such a wonderful opportunity to enhance your child's intellectual development – don't miss it! Your child will probably be very excited about the upcoming adventure of going to school; be positive and encouraging about school, even if you are a little overwhelmed at the prospect. It will be fine, and your child will enjoy the new challenge!

Chores

As we, taking the long-term view, continue to develop a *functional, independent, contributing adult,* consider giving your child a few chores at this age if you have not already done so. Preschoolers can pick up their toys, match socks when you do laundry, help to set the table, help to carry groceries, and help to care for the family pet. It may be helpful to make a game or song for "cleanup time" to smooth the process along. Many children take pride in their ability to help at this age, and they should get in the habit of contributing to the family unit from this age onward. Even if your child does not desire to do any chores, you should still see that the child completes his or her assigned tasks; we are also working to develop your child's work ethic as well as teaching basic life skills.

Your preschooler should be dressing and undressing him or herself, brushing teeth morning and night, and can begin to take showers if you'd like. My husband conducted a "fireman" drill every morning to speed up the dressing process, and the kids loved racing against the clock! Our kids were a little concerned about getting their faces wet in the shower at first, but they soon adjusted. You may need to conduct a few random shower inspections to be sure they are actually washing and not just playing in the water ☺. Look how *independent* your child is becoming!

Parenting Matters: Raising Successful Kids

Mealtimes

Toddlers and preschoolers can sometimes challenge parents at the dinner table. Offer a variety of healthy foods at each meal, and be sure not to allow your child to snack too close to mealtimes. Encourage your child to at least try new foods, especially vegetables, which tend to be an acquired taste. If your child is too "full" to eat a reasonable portion of healthy foods, he/she is also too "full" for dessert! Be consistent, and your child will learn to eat the majority of foods he or she is offered. You can also begin teaching rudimentary table manners, such as using utensils instead of fingers, and chewing with a closed mouth.

If you are a person of faith, your child should also begin his/her development in this area if he/she has not already done so. Your child can attend your place of worship with you, and he/she can attend Sunday School classes to learn more about your faith if they are available. Faith and values have a positive impact on your child's personality and development. Church attendance should not be the child's option at this age or even through the teen years; it is

Preschoolers

best if the whole family attends church as a unit. On the way home from church, I would ask the kids what they learned in church or in Sunday School; this reinforced their learning and gave them the opportunity to articulate and summarize the ideas presented, enhancing their communication skills.

Parenting Matters: Raising Successful Kids

Chapter Five: Elementary School Age

The first day of school is here! Be sure to get that picture of them boarding the school bus on the first day of school! Riding the school bus is another step towards *independence,* so let your child enjoy the adventure. I'm sure you shopped for that back-to-school outfit and backpack, along with the supplies on the supply list. Be supportive and show confidence in your child's abilities as your child starts school – your child will be in very competent hands.

Homework

Even kindergarten children may have homework. Now is the time to encourage personal responsibility in your child. Answer questions and ensure that homework is correct and complete, but do not do the child's homework for him! School is his/her job, and good work habits start early. Assignments should be completed accurately and on time. Be prepared to help your child with vocabulary words and math facts such as the times tables (flashcards are great tools for this!). Speaking of math facts, please use those flash cards, or software of your choice, at appropriate times during the elementary years to teach your child his/her addition, subtraction, multiplication and division facts; as a counselor, I have seen many students struggle in math classes in secondary school because these basic math facts were not mastered during the elementary years. Consistent repetition will really make a difference!

Children need a regular time and place to do homework each evening; see that your child gets in the habit of completing assignments and studying for tests and quizzes each school day afternoon in a quiet location. Even at this young age, it is important to provide motivation for homework completion by talking with your child about the importance of his/her education as well as your educational goals for your child, such as attending college.

Elementary School Age

School Communication

In elementary school, many teachers provide a weekly syllabus to help parents supervise homework completion; in secondary school, the syllabus normally is sent home once a year at the beginning of the school year. Please read all school communications, especially newsletters, to know what events are upcoming (conference dates, report cards, testing, school closings, enrichment opportunities), and mark your calendar accordingly so that your child's activities are not forgotten in the busyness of everyday life.

Parents should attend back-to-school night and parent-teacher conference meetings each year, and should review report cards each grading period to monitor the child's progress and address problem areas as they arise. I remember a phone call from a parent during my first year as a school counselor; in the month of May, the parent called to tell me that she hadn't seen a report card all school year! Now of course any child that withholds a report card is wrong, but a parent that waits until May to inquire about the child's progress is not paying enough attention to the child's educational process. As a parent, one *must* be aware of report card dates; please call the school and check if the date comes and your child does not bring home a report card.

Parent-Teacher Conferences

Parent-teacher conferences are a golden opportunity to meet face-to-face with the people who teach your child each day – don't miss them! I always attended back-to-school night so that I could have the teacher associate a face with my name; I listened to each teacher's presentation, introduced myself, and asked the teacher to please contact me if he or she had any concerns with my child. The first parent-teacher conference of the school year is also an event not to be missed; the teacher(s) provide essential feedback that can be used to improve your child's performance in school. Your presence at these events communicates your concern for your child's education and your expectations for your child's performance. Please establish and maintain good communication with your child's teacher(s) through open house events, back-to-school nights,

Elementary School Age

conferences, and email. Your support of the education process is critical; the teacher cannot do it alone. Your child's educational success will be a result of a team effort – the teacher, the parent, and the student. Is this a lot of work? Yes, it is. Is it worth it? You bet it is!!! A good education is priceless, and it does not happen without parental support!!!

School day mornings can be hectic for everyone! Book bags with completed homework assignments should be packed before bedtime, so that completed work is not left behind in the morning rush. Setting out clothing for the next day and packing school lunches the night before are also steps that make for smoother, less hectic mornings. Speaking of mornings – introduce your child to an alarm clock during the elementary years, so that he/she can become accustomed to rising with the alarm or music; it amazes me to see high school students whose parents still get them up each morning! This is another opportunity to help your child along the road to *independence*. If necessary, put the alarm clock across the room rather than beside the bed if hitting the "snooze" button is a problem, or if the alarm is ignored altogether! ☺

Parenting Matters: Raising Successful Kids

School Attendance

Never underestimate the power of being there! Attending school every day is essential to your child's success; minimize absences so that your child does not miss valuable instruction time. Parents should make every effort to schedule vacations, ski trips, visits to the state fair, and timeshare stays during times when school is not in session so that your child does not fall behind in school. Doctor and dentist visits should be scheduled outside of school hours for the same reason; it is easier to keep up than to catch up!

Another key concept is that you should make every effort not to have your child change schools during the school year, especially if it means moving out of state. Parents sometimes think that "school is school is school", but schools are not all doing the same thing at the same time! Schools can offer different class options even in the same school district, and schools in different areas teach particular subject areas at different times. Students who repeatedly change schools during the school year may miss key concepts and experience difficulties in school.

School Behavior

Behavior issues have a tremendous impact on students' academic performance; time missed from the classroom due to suspensions also means missed instructional time – remember the power of being there! Please let your child know that good behavior at school is expected, and that he or she is to respect the teacher's authority in school, along with letting you, the parent, know if there are any problems at school. Parents should also give teachers the benefit of the doubt if there are concerns; most teachers are experienced professionals who have your child's best interest at heart. When you have the opportunity, speak positively about your child's teachers, administrators, coaches, and other adult authority figures your child encounters – it will make a difference in your child's perception of these important people in his or her life.

Parenting Matters: Raising Successful Kids

Peer relationships gain importance during the school-age years. Continue to supervise your child outside of school hours, and don't be afraid to discourage inappropriate friendships if necessary. Your child should obtain your permission to play inside someone else's home, and you as the parent should ensure that proper supervision is in place; exercise caution, and only extend this privilege if you know the parents very well and are sure they share your values. Talk with your child about his or her day, and be alert to changes in your child's mood or demeanor. Encourage your child to have respect for self and others, and notify your child's teacher if your child is being bullied at school.

Chores

Continue to have your child complete age-appropriate chores around the house; if you have not begun to have your child help around the house, now is the time! School-age kids can set the table, pick up their toys, help with dishes, laundry, and yard work, and run the vacuum, so get them involved in contributing to the household. They will begin to learn valuable self-care skills necessary to being a

Elementary School Age

functional, independent, contributing adult, and you will have help with some of your domestic responsibilities. This is especially important when both parents work outside the home, but it is valuable even if one parent is at home full-time. Sometimes children will dawdle or even do a poor job at a chore in an attempt to get you to come to the rescue, relieving them of their responsibilities; don't fall for this trick – be patient and determined to teach your child these basic living skills.

Activities

Your child should begin or continue to participate in sports, music, community service opportunities, the arts, and other activities outside the home based on his/her interests. These outlets provide additional opportunities for children to build their self-esteem, make a contribution to the community, and have fun! One caveat – don't overdo it with outside activities. School is your child's primary responsibility, so be sure adequate time is allowed for homework completion and proper rest; also, children need unstructured downtime to relax and play just as adults do, so avoid overscheduling your child (and yourself!). With three kids, one sport per kid per season was our guideline.

Sports

Participation in sports helps your child learn teamwork, responsibility, and how to graciously win and lose; sports participation can also be the beginning point for a lifetime commitment to fitness. If you decide to have your child participate in sports, attend practices with your child to see what drills and activities are being taught; on days when your child does not have practices or games, you should reinforce those drills by practicing with your child at home. This reinforcement will help your child's skills develop and will increase your child's enjoyment of the sport. Your presence at practice also provides supervision for coaches and allows you to observe (and correct, if necessary) your child's behavior at practice. We thought it was important for our kids to learn to finish what they started, so once we paid for a season of a sport, the children finished the season even if they wanted to quit; often, they learned to enjoy the sport more as their skill level improved. Both parents, if possible, should be involved in the child's academic and sports training at home. We went with our strengths – I primarily handled academics and my husband primarily handled sports, although we helped out in both areas as needed.

The Arts

My children also enjoyed participation in music and the arts, primarily through school activities, but sometimes supplemented with private lessons as they fit the family budget and schedule. Your child's own talents and interests are great indicators of options to pursue. Community activities such as the children's choir at church are also great ways to incorporate the arts into your child's experiences, as well as visits to the museums and performances of your choice. My husband and I took the children to see the Nutcracker ballet each year at Christmas, and it has become a well-loved family tradition that continues to this day with the grandchildren.

Media Supervision

Parents of elementary school children should use the parental lock functions available on cable and satellite TV to ensure that their children are not exposed to inappropriate content. Investigate and use parental controls for your computer as well. Part of the parental role is to ensure that your child is not exposed to too much, too soon; proper supervision and parental controls are part of that job. Also be cautious about giving your child a cell phone too quickly; ours did not use one until they had their driver's licenses and drove around without us, and they did not own one until college.

Latchkey Kids

As your child approaches middle school age, you may find that your child wants to come home after school instead of going to a daycare when both parents work. The legal age when children can come home varies, and developmentally speaking, children are ready for this level of responsibility at different ages, but when you are

Elementary School Age

ready for your child to be a "latchkey" kid, here are a few rules for him/her to follow (I posted them on the door in our family room for easy reference):

- Come directly inside the house after you get off the school bus.
- No one is allowed inside your house other than the people who live there.
- Lock the door once inside the house.
- Call Mom/Dad to let us know you are home safely.
- Relax/snack/watch TV for thirty minutes.
- Begin your homework and keep working until a parent comes home.
- No fighting! Call Mom/Dad with any disputes.

All of my kids were "latchkey" kids at one time or another, and they handled it well, staying within the rules. I did have the occasional opportunity to settle disputes over the phone ☺, and my husband and I did specify which snacks were permissible for those after-school munchies. Of course, if the phone rings, they should not tell strangers that their parents are not home; if you have "caller id", your kids should not even answer the phone unless they know the caller well (primarily just parents and grandparents). It is also a good idea to establish a "safe house" where your kids can go if there is an emergency, such as the door being ajar when they get home, forgetting their house key, etc. This should be a trusted neighbor who will be home at that time of day, and your kids still need to call you so you know where they are and why. Your child is taking another step towards becoming a *functional, independent, contributing adult!*

Chapter Six: Tweens (Middle School)

Academics, Part II

Can you believe your child is in middle school already? As we leave elementary school behind, new challenges present themselves at a new level. The biggest difference is that your child now has multiple teachers and is now changing classes. Your child now needs to **write down his assignments for each class** so that he/she can complete homework and projects on time and study for tests and quizzes as necessary. Writing down assignments and completing them daily is a critical skill for success at the middle school and high school levels and beyond into college and the world of work. Parents can help in the development of this habit by checking to see that the assignments have been recorded each day; as the skill is mastered, an occasional spot-check will ensure that this essential habit remains in place. This one habit, along with doing the assignments that are written down, will greatly impact your child's grades for the remainder of his/her educational career. Also, please continue to attend parent-teacher conferences, monitor report cards, and email your child's teachers as necessary to ensure your child's progress in school. This effort is even more essential now that your child has multiple teachers and subjects in school! As a school counselor, I have seen that students who struggle in high school are usually those that did not lay this groundwork in middle school; make your life and your child's life easier by rising to the challenge now!!!

Tweens Expectations

It is important to discuss your academic expectations with your child, along with the consequences that will ensue if expectations are not met. If your goal is for your child to get and stay on the honor roll and you are providing the necessary support (e.g. checking for written assignments each day, knowing when interims and report cards are due and reviewing them, attending parent-teacher conferences, and contacting teachers whenever your child struggles), your child should be aware of this expectation, and there can be rewards and consequences to help your child achieve

Tweens (Middle School)

these academic goals. Some parents hope it is sufficient to simply ask their children if school is going well, if they have done their homework, and if they are making good grades. Please be aware that children, even your precious angel, will lie in an attempt to avoid trouble. There is no substitute for insisting to see completed homework assignments and report cards, as well as remaining in communication with teachers through conferences and emails. You don't want unfortunate surprises in this area, so be warned!

It is also important to maintain academic momentum during the summer months. If your child is not in a formal summer program, encourage him/her to read during the summer, and seek materials online or at local stores that will reinforce what he/she has learned, especially in the areas of mathematics and foreign language; these academic areas are especially dependent upon previous learning for future success.

Parenting Matters: Raising Successful Kids

Tweens Fashion

If your tween has not been bitten by the fashion bug, rest assured that he or she will be! It can be a challenge to navigate these waters, but you will make it! Some parents abdicate and let the tween wear whatever he/she likes, but while that is the easy path, it is not necessarily the best one. As the parent you can veto clothing that has inappropriate messages, is too revealing, or is otherwise unsuitable. It is also not necessary to go broke outfitting tweens and teens! We told them what we could reasonably afford to spend for back-to-school shopping and went with them to shop (note, we did *not* drop them off at the mall to shop unsupervised with friends), after we explained that this was all the money that would be available to them. If they chose to spend their total allotment on one pair of expensive sneakers and an equally expensive pair of jeans, they would have to live with that decision. This plan introduces the idea of a budget and of being fiscally responsible, which fits nicely into our goal of raising a *functional, independent, contributing adult!* By the way, it is advisable not to drop tweens off at the mall and leave them unsupervised; they can be encouraged by their friends to shoplift, and they are at the mercy of older teens/adults who may not be appropriate influences on your precious child. We found that our children best handled this level of responsibility when they were old enough to drive themselves to the mall.

Tweens Transition

Please note that while your child can be reasonably fashionable, extremes in appearance at the middle school or high school level can sometimes make your child a target for bullies, so aim for an appearance in the mainstream that both you and your tween can agree upon. Wearing black from head to toe may not be the best attire for your tween; aim for a look that does not draw undue attention. Another thing to note is that your little boy who previously hated bathtime will now be taking two or three showers a day, will tie his shoes without a reminder from you, and will probably leave the house in a cloud of cologne or after-shave. Pretty wild, huh??? ☺ This interesting behavior can result from the sudden awareness of the opposite sex. Tweens are going through a period of rapid change, and they can be a little spacey during this transition –

especially during the first year of middle school. Mine left book bags in my car (only remembered when I was on the opposite side of town at work ☹), forgot choral attire on the day of the concert, and sometimes remembered projects due Monday morning at 10:00 pm Sunday night, necessitating a late-night run to the store for poster board and supplies (until we learned to stock up on those items for just such an occasion ☺). Hang in there – this transition will pass and things will improve on many fronts. I should also warn you that parents of tweens may go from being your child's hero to a less desirable status as their peer relationships take center stage. Don't be hurt – they still love you but they are growing up, and this is also a natural transition.

Tweens and Money

If you have not established an allowance for your child, this is a good time to begin. Your child can spend his own money for toys, games, clothing, and treats, so that he/she learns to make choices and live within a budget. And since you are hopefully shopping with your child at the store and providing the necessary supervision, you can ensure that his or her choices of toys, games, and clothing meet your standards. Whether or not you attend a church, your child should get into the habit of making regular charitable donations from his/her own funds. It is also a good idea to open a savings account for your child if you have not already done so, and encourage/require your child to save monetary gifts, earned income, and some of his/her allowance for future needs and wants.

Tweens Activities

Extracurricular activities continue to be important for tweens, and school-related activities often replace or supplement those available in the community. Our kids played a school-related sport most seasons in middle school and in high school; not only does this open the door for athletic scholarships for college, but it is a productive social outlet, it provides supervision during after-school hours, and it develops lifelong habits of working out and staying active. As your tween enters the world of competitive sports teams, encourage him or her to first concentrate on making the team; the secondary goal is to get into the starting lineup, and the final goal is to start at the child's preferred position, such as shortstop in baseball or safety in football. And please continue to support your child's athletic efforts by attending his or her sporting events and cheering for the home team!

Tweens and Media Concerns

Parents of tweens should continue to have boundaries for movie viewing as well as telephone, TV and computer use. It is best to avoid phones, TVs and computers in the child's bedroom where possible. In this day of laptops and cell phones, it is very difficult for parents to monitor technology use, but the goal is for technology use to be in a more "public" area of your home where you can supervise what shows are watched on TV (TV programs have a useful rating system for parents to use), what websites are being visited on the computer, and when telephone conversations take place. Your supervision is your best tool available, along with discussing your expectations with your child. You may need to "hold" your child's cell phone during the nighttime hours if your child wants to talk and/or text all night long! Investigate and use parental controls for your televisions and your computers; unfortunately, the advance of technology has increased the potential exposure of our children to inappropriate content. Concerning movies, we found it best to enforce the rating system already in place, e.g. not taking 13-year-olds to see "R" rated movies; this also applies to movies they see in your home or elsewhere.

Tweens and Sexual Activity

I don't know any parents who think that tweens should engage in sexual activity, but there are pregnant middle schoolers, so clearly some of them are doing so! If you haven't had "the talk" with your tween, please do so immediately!! Yes, they do have "family life" education in school, but they need to hear from you concerning relationships, sex, birth control, STDs, and what you consider appropriate behavior and boundaries. It was our goal for our kids to remain abstinent as long as possible, until marriage or at least until the college years, so we provided all the supervision we could and kept them as busy and engaged in activities as was feasible, the goal being to limit their opportunities to make decisions in this area that they would later regret. We declined invitations for our kids to attend co-ed sleepovers, and if they had friends over, the visiting occurred in "public" areas of the house such as the family room, where we could walk through occasionally to keep an eye on them. Visitors also had to leave by a reasonable hour. Being a grandparent is a wonderful thing, but not while your child is in middle school or high school and is still living with you!!

Tweens and Authority

Tweens can be expected to periodically challenge your authority; expect opposition and stand strong!! You may even need to utter the words you thought you never would use: "Because I said so" ☺ As kids we hated that phrase, but as parents we know that children will neither agree with nor understand all the decisions parents make and the rules parents put in place; the child must do as the parent says because the parent has greater knowledge and experience and, more importantly, the parent is responsible for the child. As the parent, you will gradually grant your child more freedom at the pace you deem appropriate; more than likely, your child will not agree with your pace. This is totally normal and can be expected to last until your child actually leaves home. ☺

Tweens may look more "grown up" than elementary school kids, but they still need substantial monitoring and discipline from their parents. One particularly good punishment at this age was called "double chores"; this only works if a) your children do household chores, as has been previously advised, and b) if you have more than one child. When child A commits a rules infraction, he or she must do not only his chores but the chores of child B for a specified period. We had three kids, so major infractions resulted in "triple chores", to the chagrin of the misbehaving child and to the delight of the others!! Both "double chores" and "triple chores" were very effective punishments in our household.

Family Time

Much attention has been paid to the idea of the family eating dinner together. This goal gets more difficult to meet as your children get older and have more and more demands on their time; I encourage you to continue to make the effort to eat dinner together as often as possible, and on occasion, have what we called a "family forum". This meeting, usually over dinner, is an opportunity for each family member to discuss topics of concern. We would talk about daily events, grievances, future plans, perceived inequities, and any problems the kids had with the parents or vice versa. This time was also a teachable moment to discuss our values, faith, and character issues such as tolerance, honesty, and trust. If you haven't had a "family forum", initiate one soon!

If you really love your children, you will continue to protect them, guide them, and insist that good choices are made, even when those choices are not popular, and even though it would be easier to go down the "wide path" and let them do whatever they choose. Remember that their outcomes are dependent on your choices; don't let them down now!!!

As you can see, parenting of tweens (and teens) is very challenging, to say the least. And you thought the "terrible twos" were difficult!!! These are critical years in your child's

Tweens (Middle School)

development, and will require your full attention. Hang in there – we are making progress towards our goal!

Parenting Matters: Raising Successful Kids

Chapter Seven: Teens (High School)

Academic Concerns

High school is a different world! With the increased freedom of high school life comes increased responsibility. All of your child's grades now count on their permanent record. If you have been following the advice from previous chapters, your child already possesses the work ethic and organizational skills to be academically successful in the high school setting. Your child needs to continue to write down assignments each day and complete them, as well as studying for tests and quizzes and completing projects as assigned. Daily school attendance is still essential. And as the parent, you still need to attend back-to-school night and parent-teacher conferences, check interim grades and report cards, and email teachers as necessary to ensure your child's academic success. It is also essential that you continue to be accessible to your child's school and teachers; return phone calls, promptly attend to paperwork that comes home, and be sure the school always has up-to-date contact

Parenting Matters: Raising Successful Kids

information so that you can be reached as needed by school personnel. Your child is taller and looks more mature, but he/she will continue to need you to support him/her and to set appropriate boundaries.

Academically, your child should be taking challenging classes, such as advanced, Advanced Placement (AP), and International Baccalaureate (IB) courses, especially if his/her goal is a selective college; these advanced classes build a strong foundation for college-level work, and can improve your child's grade point average (GPA). Your child should continue to be involved in sports, clubs, and other activities at school and in the community, seeking leadership roles in the activities of his/her choice. College-bound high school students should take PSAT, SAT and/or ACT tests by the end of the junior year; they should visit potential colleges as time permits (spring break of the junior year is a great time to do this!), and submit college applications during the fall of the senior year. Your child may need assistance with organizing and prioritizing all the activities on his/her plate; your support with this time management effort will be essential in most cases for your child's success.

Working

There will also be some new challenges for you to maneuver as the parent of a teen: dating, driving, curfews, prom, beach week, college applications, and working. Let's start with working. We are in favor of teens working during the summer months; working will teach them valuable life lessons and give them more income to manage. Our kids worked every summer during their high school years; half the money they earned went into their savings accounts for use when they left home, and the other half they could spend, with the understanding that they were now responsible for their own back-to-school wardrobe. The teen years are also a great time for children to open a checking account and get a debit card (we did this around the age of sixteen or so); the teen will have the opportunity to learn how to balance a checking account, use a debit card, and write checks so that they are proficient money managers by the time they graduate high school. Since they will have income, they will also need to learn how to file an income tax return; for most teens this is simply completing the "short form" and collecting a tax refund!

Our kids did not have regular employment during the school year, since they took challenging classes and participated in high school sports, music, and the arts in the afternoons; they did babysit during the school year for "pocket money". While working is an important step towards becoming a *functional, independent, contributing adult,* you must ensure that school remains your child's primary responsibility; he will have many years of adulthood to work. Many teens work lots of hours during the school year to pay for a car and car insurance, and their grades suffer as a result; it is best for high school students not to work more than 20 hours per week during the school year so that they have adequate time for homework, school attendance, and proper rest.

Driving

Driving is a very important teen rite of passage. There are few things quite as challenging as teaching your teen how to drive, and you have our prayers and sympathy! One of my favorite sayings for my kids as they grew up was, "with freedom comes responsibility" – this is certainly true of the freedom drivers enjoy! New drivers are very distractible and prone to accidents, so we did not allow our new drivers to transport anyone other than family members for the first 12 months that they possessed a driver's license. It is scary enough having your own children at the mercy of an inexperienced driver – we thought it wise not to risk the safety of anyone else's children until our young drivers gained considerable experience on the road! We did not buy a car for the young drivers; they drove one of the family cars. In this way, it was clear that we controlled their driving privileges, and it was reasonable for us to set expectations for the use of our car. We gave each child a car (not a new car, but what we could afford) as a present when they graduated college; then the car, car insurance, maintenance, and related expenses were totally their own!

Parenting Matters: Raising Successful Kids

Dating

Dating is another challenging arena. Often tweens go on "group dates", but teens want to progress to individual dates. If you have still not had the "birds and bees" talk, you had better do so now! Be sure your child knows your expectations and beliefs concerning relationships and sex. You may also want to give your teen a few condoms; it is a bit of a mixed message, since we weren't encouraging them to be sexually active at this age, but we felt that the consequences of unprotected sex were so serious, we wanted to be sure they were protected if they chose to be sexually active. It is also important for there to be an itinerary for the date – don't allow your children to go "out" with no idea of where they will be or what they will be doing at this stage of the game (that is college-level freedom!).

If your child is being transported by another teen for the date, the other teen should come in your home and meet you, so that you have the opportunity to meet the person to whom you are entrusting your child's safety. If your child is attending a party at another

Teens (High School)

teen's house, contact the parents in advance to ensure that they will be chaperoning the event before you let your child attend. As the parent, it is still your job to keep your child as safe as you can; this includes protection from situations they are not yet ready to handle.

Curfew

Have a curfew established for your child, and be clear about the time your child is to return home. The natural punishment for curfew violations was temporary suspension of dating privileges, so our kids did their best to be home on time! Our children did not normally date on school nights, since they were participating in sports and had homework to complete. If you decide to allow dating during the school week, your child's curfew should be earlier than on the weekend so that your child can be awake and learning during the school day. Exceptions can be made to the normal curfew for special events like the prom.

It can be wise to occasionally check to see if your teens are where they tell you they are, whether it is sports practice or a date to the mall. Perhaps you can arrive at a pickup point earlier than agreed upon to see if your child is really at that sports practice or mall! Any child can be tempted to lie to their parents about their whereabouts, so don't be shocked if this happens – they're only human. However, it is important for them to know that you are checking on them.

Room Checks

By the way, you should periodically check your children's rooms to be sure they are in bed at night; also check their rooms when they are not home to ensure that they have not adopted any bad habits such as drugs and alcohol. Early intervention is key in these situations! Finally, be sure your child knows that underage drinking is both illegal and a bad idea, since drinking has been shown to be detrimental to brain development for teens; drunk driving is another topic for you and your child to discuss. Toddlers are challenging, but the teen years are the real challenge period in parenting!!!

Teens (High School)

College Applications

Senior year is an exciting time, with college applications to complete, prom on the agenda, and the beach week decision. It is essential for parents to be involved in the college application process; teens have good intentions, but often lack the ability to manage the process and meet application deadlines. A good goal is to finish and submit all the college applications by Thanksgiving; submitting applications early can maximize your children's chances for financial aid, and will have this demanding phase completed before the very busy holiday season of decorating, shopping, concerts, family gatherings, and other activities. We had great, disciplined kids, but **all three** had to be grounded until they submitted their college applications! Parents, you and your teen have worked hard to get to this point – assert your authority to ensure that they make it to the finish line! However, do not complete the applications for them. You will not be going to college with them, and they need to handle this process with your encouragement and support; proofread the essays, but don't write them for your teen. If essays are not your strong point, your child's

English teacher is a great person to ask for proofreading help. If your teen is not ready for college-level responsibility, it is better and cheaper for you to find that out now instead of after you have spent college tuition that will not be refunded if your child does not rise to the challenge of producing college-level work on his or her own. And parents, you will have your opportunity to contribute to the college application process; the FAFSA form must be completed by parents and students starting in January of the senior year in order for students to qualify for financial aid for college.

Options after High School

Of course, every high school graduate will not be going away to college; some will continue to live at home and attend community college, perhaps transferring to a four-year institution at a future time depending on the student's career plans. Still others will go into military service, and some will go directly into the world of work. It is important for parents to encourage their children to work towards *independence* after their high school days are done. A friend of ours said that his father taped a note to his bedroom mirror during his senior year listing his options after graduation: college, the military, or moving out! ☺ Certainly the point needs to be made that an extended adolescence, e.g., staying home indefinitely with no exit strategy, is not an option for your child.

Prom and Beach Week

Prom (and after-prom) is a very special time for your teen; check their itinerary for the evening, and emphasize them getting home safely! We didn't allow our kids to attend beach week because of supervision concerns, but if you allow yours to go, again emphasize safety and personal responsibility. We felt that it was best to allow college-level freedoms, such as a week unsupervised with other teens, once they were actually in college. Be warned that your child will not like this decision; we told ours well in advance so that they knew what to expect.

Parenting Matters: Raising Successful Kids

Your Child and 18

One final word for this very challenging stage: on turning 18! Somehow teenagers often have the mistaken idea that once they turn 18, they no longer have to do anything their parents tell them. Talk to your kids prior to their 18th birthday and help them understand that they are not independent, self-determining adults until they pay all their own bills and live elsewhere! If they plan to continue living under your roof and/or depending upon you for financial support, they need to continue to respect your authority. Indeed, rightly understood, a child turning 18 is an advantage for the parents, who are no longer legally obligated to support them after their 18th birthday. Remind them of this fact as necessary, and congratulations on reaching this stage of the journey!

Chapter Eight: College and Beyond

Wow, you survived some of the toughest stages of parenting, and you have almost achieved the empty nest! Your child has graduated high school, but there are still a few challenges before you cross the finish line. Young adults are still developing adult judgment, and they have much to learn. Some topics to discuss with your child are handling money, credit cards, cell phones, and other expenses. If you have not discussed budgeting with your child, now is the time! Your child should list his/her expenses and ensure that his/her cash flow is sufficient to cover them; this applies whether your child is going to college or getting a job and moving out on his/her own.

Credit and Debit Cards

Be sure your young adult avoids incurring lots of credit card debt, especially while they are full-time students with limited income. A friend's child ran up so much credit card debt in college, the child had to take several semesters off from school to work and pay off the debt! Encourage your child to use a debit card instead so that they spend within their means; this also means that they should be managing their checking account so that they don't have expensive overdrafts. They should consider pay-as-you-go cell phones to minimize their expenses from talking and texting; expenditures for books, clothing, and meals out should be planned so that their expenses do not exceed their income. Any assistance or allowance you plan to give them should be a part of their budgeted income. Don't just give your child your credit card; this is the time of life for them to learn that money does not grow on trees, and that fiscally sound adults manage their money. Each of our kids spent their personal cash pretty rapidly during their first semester of college; resist the parental urge to rush to their rescue! Their bills are paid, and they have food (the meal plan) and shelter – they will be fine, and they will learn from the experience if you let them. Our kids worked each summer during college to replenish their personal cash, and they spent more wisely in subsequent school years.

College and Beyond

College Visits

Of course you will miss your child, but please don't drop by to visit unannounced! Arrange your visits with your children in advance – they have their own, new lives now that they are away from home. Your child should be encouraged to remain at school for the first month or two without coming home on the weekends, so that he/she can become accustomed to living *independently,* which would include doing his/her own laundry! ☺ My oldest son's college encouraged parents to give the new college student his/her space until Parents' Weekend in late October. Your child may be a little homesick at first, but coming home every weekend will only prolong the adjustment process. Given time, your child will make new friends and thrive in his/her new environment.

Summer Break

The first summer your children come back home from college can be interesting as well. They have become accustomed to adult freedoms, but there can be conflicts when they return home for school breaks. The key is to allow more freedom (no particular curfew, perhaps), but for the parents to still have a general idea of the child's whereabouts (e.g., their destination and route), out of concern for their safety. College students often operate on a completely different schedule from working adults, so your child may be used to loud music and TV at all hours! This schedule may work in a dormitory but can be problematic in your home; you and your child may need to agree upon times to reduce the noise level.

Post-College Transition

Before you know it, the college experience will wind down, and your child will be ready for the next phase – graduate school or the job search. Be supportive but encourage your child to take the lead in the process. I've heard of parents these days actually going on job interviews with their children – this is totally inappropriate, and can sabotage your child's efforts! If you have been following the ideas in this book, your child will be ready for the challenges he or she will face in the work world. If your adult child needs to live with you for a while, I suggest you charge rent, assign household chores, and implement house rules, such as no overnight guests; the idea is to help him/her see the advantages of having his/her own place!! At long last, the empty nest will finally be a reality – congratulations on raising a *functional, independent, contributing adult*!!

Parenting Matters: Raising Successful Kids

Chapter Nine: Parenting In a Nutshell

Boundaries, Rules, Authority, and Discipline are concepts that are avoided by many modern-day parents; these same parents sit in my school counselor's office at work and wonder why their child is not performing well in school, or why their child has so much trouble at school, where there are authority figures, and no trouble at home, where the child is permitted to do pretty much whatever he/she wants. The reality parents need to face is that the society in which we live has rules, laws, and authority; schools and workplaces will have people in authority, and children must accustom themselves to handling boundaries, rules, and authority. And remember that discipline is not the enemy of enthusiasm! Parents must love their children enough to discipline them.

Teamwork and Work Ethic are themes that begin when your children are young and continue throughout their time with you. They are both closely linked to the discipline concept, since work often involves completing a task or activity that you would not choose to do. Once your child learns to join other family members in a task as part of a team, or learns to complete independent household chores and schoolwork, he/she has a valuable tool that will serve him/her for the rest of his/her life.

Parental Sacrifice has been implied throughout this book, but it should be explicitly stated as a requirement as well. From when they are small to when they are tall, children require supervision, love, money and time. It will take considerable energy and resources (time, money, attention) to raise good kids, and your children will have to be a priority in terms of job choices and external activities. Remember that you have *only one* opportunity to raise your children, and *multiple* opportunities to attain many other goals and participate in many other activities. Your children are depending on you to make the right choice!!

Protection of your child/tween/teen is a primary parental responsibility. Your supervision and rules protect your child from the very real dangers they face in today's world. Our children felt that we were overprotective. Our response was that they were priceless to us; if we had to choose between being overprotective and being underprotective, we were choosing to be overprotective. So many troubling experiences cannot be undone, and your child will have opportunities to experience whatever they wish to experience when they are fully grown and on their own; those "missed" opportunities will present themselves again, when your child is a young adult and better able to handle those challenges. Getting your child to adulthood with no major bumps or traumatic events is a major accomplishment!!

Parenting Matters: Raising Successful Kids

Chapter Ten: Frequently Asked Questions

1) How should parents handle bullying?

If your child reports bullying at school or on the school bus, you should contact the administrators at your child's school for assistance. For problems with friends or neighbors, discuss the issues with the other child's parents (for younger children), or encourage your child to talk calmly with the other child in an attempt to work out their differences. Sometimes it is best for the children not to associate with each other for a while if the issues cannot be resolved. Most of us have experienced bullying on some level, and from that experience we learn how careful we should be in interacting with others.

2) Do these ideas apply equally to boys and girls?

I didn't have daughters, but my parents used many of these ideas in raising me. I have also seen parents of girls use these same techniques with success. Both boys and girls need to become *functional, independent, contributing adults* – men and women who will make you proud!

3) What do you do when you are just tired and don't feel like being a good parent?

My suggestion is to take a day off from work to rest and rejuvenate yourself; you might also get a babysitter and plan a night out, or take the kids to Grandma's for a day or a weekend. This may also be the time to examine your schedule and determine if some activities or responsibilities need to be deferred or dropped so that you can have the energy to be a good parent while you have the opportunity to do so.

4) What changes would you make for single parents, or when one parent travels a lot?

As a single parent (in practicality or in reality), you will need a strong support system of friends and relatives to help out on the

Frequently Asked Questions

parenting journey. Seek supporters who share your views on discipline, academic achievement, and other parenting issues.

5) How does the parents' marriage influence the child's development?

Parental relationships are watched closely and often modeled by children. I have counseled many children who were deeply affected by parents who tolerated mistreatment or abuse from their significant others. Please seek individual, couples, or family counseling if your home's atmosphere is a stressful one for the children.

6) Have these principles worked with children other than your own?

Yes, yes, and yes! We are hardly the only parents to follow this model. Over the years we have known many parents who have employed these guidelines and had consistent success raising their children.

7) What if I do all of this and fail?

There are no guarantees in life, so of course it is possible to do all you can as a parent but still not get the desired outcome. When you look back and know that you have done the best you could do as a parent, you have more peace about the results, whatever they are.

Topical Index

Academic concerns and teens	73
Academic concerns and tweens	59
Activities - school age children	53
Activities - tweens	65
Arts - school age children	55
Authority and tweens	68
Babies, independent play of	26
Baby's first days	23
Beach week	83
Behavior of school age children	51
Bullying of school age children	52, 95
Bullying of tweens	63 ,95
Chores - preschoolers	40
Chores - school age children	52
College applications	81
College summer	87
College visits	87
Credit/Debit cards	85
Curfew	79

Parenting Matters: Raising Successful Kids

Dad's involvement	25
Dating - teens	78
Do's for toddlers	34
Driving - teens	76
Expectations for tweens	60
Family time	69
Fashion and tweens	62
Future options - teens	82
Homework	45
Independence, babies and	26
Latchkey kids	56
Mealtimes	42
Media concerns - school age children	56
Media concerns - tweens	66
Money and tweens	64
Nighttime preparation	49
Parent-teacher conferences	48
Post college transition	88
Potty training	36
Preschoolers and why	40
Prom	83
Room checks	80

Topical Index

School attendance, importance of	50
School communication	47
Sexual activity - tweens	67
Sports - school age children	54
Temper tantrums	32
Toddler do's	34
Turning 18	84
Tweens and academics	59
Tweens and authority	68
Tweens and expectations	60
Tweens and fashion	62
Tweens and money	64
Why and preschoolers	40
Working - teens	75

About the Author

Margaret Roane is a professional school counselor from Mechanicsville, Virginia. She began her career as a programmer analyst and an auditor before completing her master's degree in Counseling and transitioning to the field of education. She and her husband Vincent are the proud parents of three sons – George, a co-founder and CFO of an energy company, Randy, an assistant professor of biomedical engineering, and Joseph, a graduate teaching assistant and coaching intern.

Made in the USA
San Bernardino, CA
09 May 2014